A GUIDE

TO THE MONSTERS

OF THE MIND

VICTOR GRENKO

First published in 1991 by The Gatehouse Project.

Text & drawings copyright c Victor Grenko
Designed by Victor Grenko & Gatehouse Project
Design Consultants Saleem Zaidi, Dave Leech
Lettering Dave Leech
Gatehouse Logo Sarah Maher
Typeset by Arena
Printed by Manchester Free Press

Published and distributed by
The Gatehouse Project
St Luke's
Sawley Road
Manchester M10 8DB

Gatehouse gratefully acknowledges financial assistance from
The Association of Greater Manchester Authorities
Imperial Chemical Industries PLC
The Judith Gray Trust
Manchester & Salford Students' Rag
MIND National Association for Mental Health
North West Arts
Sandoz Pharmaceuticals
SANE (Schizophrenia, A National Emergency)

British Library Cataloguing in Publication Data
Grenko, Victor
A guide to the monsters of the mind.
1. Mental health
I. Title
362.2
ISBN 0-906253-32-2

Gatehouse is a member of the Federation of Worker Writers & Community Publishers

Back cover photograph: Patricia Duffin

FOREWORD

Everybody has monsters inside their head. These monsters are the fears, worries and hangups we all have. But when you become mentally ill, the monsters take on new, grotesque shapes. Then they torment your mind and make you unhappy. Here is a Who's Who of monsters, of beasts that freely roam inside your head. All kinds of different creatures, good and funny, tragic and sad. Once we see the monsters on paper we can laugh at them, but unknown, hidden, they lurk in the dark corners of your mind. You must be able to recognise them, or risk being devoured by them. The human mind is like an attic, that we climb into and shine a torch to see what is making all that noise. This book is a torch. It can help you come to terms with those creatures of the night, those monsters of the mind.

VICTOR GRENKO

NOW LOOK AT ALL THOSE MONSTERS INSIDE PEOPLE'S HEADS

This book is like a ride on a ghost train through my mind. Maybe you'll see a joke...

THE PICASSO PICTURE

WHEN YOU ARE LABELLED AS A
PERSON WITH PROBLEMS, YOU
PAINT A DIFFERENT PICTURE OF
YOURSELF IN YOUR MIND.

THE SMOKE TORMENTOR

THIS NICOTINE FIEND MAKES YOU
WANT A CIGARETTE. IT'S TORTURE
TO DO WITHOUT A FAG AND IT
COSTS A FORTUNE TO FEED THE ADDICTION.
I THINK I'LL GIVE SMOKING UP.

THE DARK SECRET

BEWARE! DO NOT OPEN UP THIS CLOSET!
KEEP OUT OR A SKELETON MIGHT
FALL OUT.
WHAT IS YOUR DARK SECRET?

THE EARACHE

A BIT MUTT AND JEFF? STONE DEAF?
HARD OF HEARING? YOU CAN'T
HEAR WHAT I'M SAYING?
THEN YOU'VE GOT EAR ACHE.

Maybe you'll recognise
a bit of yourself...

THE JIG-SAW PIECE

LIFE IS LIKE A JIG-SAW PUZZLE, WITHOUT THE MISSING PIECE YOUR LIFE DOESN'T MAKE SENSE. YOU'RE ALWAYS SEARCHING FOR THE LAST PIECE TO MAKE YOUR LIFE COMPLETE.

THE REALITY SERGEANT

WHO TELLS YOU THE WAY IT IS. EITHER YOU SORT YOURSELF OUT, WORK HARD, DISCIPLINE YOUR LIFE, OR YOU GO DOWN THE DRAIN.

THE IMAGINARY FRIEND

DO YOU NEED A FRIEND FOR THAT GAME OF CHESS NOBODY WILL PLAY WITH YOU? LOOK NO FURTHER THAN THE IMAGINARY FRIEND. A GOOD PAL WHO SEES YOU RIGHT.

THE ANXIETY COUCH

YOU TALK TO YOURSELF BECAUSE NOBODY ELSE WILL TALK TO YOU. EVERYBODY WANTS TO TALK BUT NOBODY WANTS TO LISTEN.

Life is complicated,
but if you hug someone,
you don't need a lot of words...

THE LOW DEPRESSION

GOT THINGS ON YOUR MIND? WORRIES?
IS LIFE GETTING YOU DOWN? YOU'RE
FEELING THE DEEP DOWN DESPAIR
OF LIVING. YOU'RE ON A DOWN.
WHAT YOU NEED IS A PICK-ME-UP.

THE HATE DRAGON

HE DETESTS EVERYBODY IN THE
WORLD INCLUDING HIMSELF. HATE
FEEDS THE FLAMES OF THE DRAGON,
AS HE THROWS HIS FIRE BREATHING
TEMPER TANTRUMS.

THE TRAPPED GENIE

IS THE FEAR OF BEING TRAPPED
FOREVER. JUST WAIT TILL YOU'RE
LOCKED IN THE BATHROOM AND
YOU CAN'T GET OUT. SEND AN
S.O.S IN A BOTTLE.

THE SCREAMING MIMI

WHEN YOU CAN'T STAND IT ANY MORE,
LET IT ALL OUT IN ONE GOOD BIG YELL.
SCREECH YOUR HEAD OFF.

You need love in the world.
If you don't get it, it's hard...

THE LONELY HEART

IS ALWAYS WAITING AT THE CHURCH,
UNLOVED AND BROKEN HEARTED.
A ONE MAN BAND WHO PLAYS SOLO
LONELY, SINGLE AND ALWAYS ALONE

THE MOCKING VOICE

IS LAUGHING AT YOU, TORMENTING YOU
WITH IT'S CRUEL, MOCKING
JEERING LAUGHTER.
STOP LAUGHING AT ME.

THE FROST MAN

YOU TURN COLD TOWARDS EVERYBODY
IN THE WORLD AND BECOME UNFEELING.
YOUR EMOTIONS ARE FROZEN LIKE ICE.
YOUR HEART IS RULED BY CONTEMPT.

THE NIGHT OWL

THE BIRD OF INSOMNIACS. IT KEEPS
YOU AWAKE AT NIGHT AND DOES
NOT LET YOU GET ANY SHUT EYE.
YOU NEED YOUR FORTY WINKS.

Sometimes you feel
as if you're trapped.
As if there's no escape.
That's the way life is...

THE AMAZING MAZE

LEADS YOUR THOUGHTS INTO
A MAZE, WHERE THEY WANDER
ABOUT LOST. YOU TRY TO FIND
YOUR WAY OUT, BUT YOU ARE TRAPPED.

THE FEAR OF STRANGERS

YOU FEAR ANYBODY NEW WHO
ENTERS YOUR LIFE. YOU ONLY FEEL
HAPPY WITH THE PEOPLE YOU KNOW.

THE DOOR KEY

PUT THE KEY INTO THE DOOR,
TURN THE LOCK AND SET ME FREE.
SOMEBODY HAS LOCKED AWAY MY
MIND AND THROWN AWAY THE KEY.

THE CHILDISH TEDDY

YOU REVERT BACK TO YOUR
CHILDHOOD AND ACT LIKE A BIG KID.
IT'S TIME YOU GREW UP AND WENT
TO HIGH SCHOOL.

Some doors are
too painful to open.
You keep them closed
because you're too scared
to open them...

THE DESERT ISLAND

NO ONE IS AN ISLAND, EXCEPT WHEN NO ONE WILL SPEAK TO YOU, AND YOU FEEL ALONE LIKE ROBINSON CRUSOE MAROONED ON AN OCEAN ROCK.

THE PARENT FIXATION

YOUR DOMINANT PARENTS REIGN OVER YOUR LIFE AND YOU'D BETTER DO AS THEY SAY OR ELSE. IT'S A CASE OF PARENTS RULE O.K.!

THE PROUD PEACOCK

WHO SHRIEKS, "HOW DARE YOU DO THIS TO ME!" THIS PROUD CREATURE IS FULL OF OUTRAGEOUS PRIDE.

THE JEALOUS EYE

ALSO KNOWN AS THE GREEN EYED MONSTER WHO EYES OTHER PEOPLE'S THINGS WITH HIS GREAT BIG GREEN JEALOUS EYE OF DESIRE.

Maybe now monsters affect you.
Don't worry, because the monsters fade out.
They only affect you for a time...

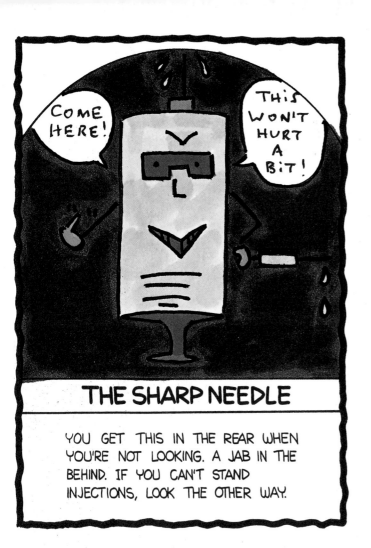

THE SHARP NEEDLE

YOU GET THIS IN THE REAR WHEN YOU'RE NOT LOOKING. A JAB IN THE BEHIND. IF YOU CAN'T STAND INJECTIONS, LOOK THE OTHER WAY.

THE LOBOTOMY BIRD

YOU FEEL YOUR MIND WILL SIMPLY FLY AWAY IF YOU ARE GIVEN A LOBOTOMY OPERATION.

THE ELECTRIC SHOCK

IS THE IDEA OF E.C.T. YOU FEEL NO PAIN, BUT THE THOUGHT OF THOSE CURRENTS GOING THROUGH YOU GIVES YOU A MILD JOLT.

THE REPEATER

UTTERS THE SAME THING OVER AND OVER AGAIN, LIKE A TAPE RECORDER GONE BERSERK. PLAY IT AGAIN SAM.

I'm just taking each day
as it comes...

THE NIGHTMARE HORSE

IF YOU DON'T FANCY A RIDE ON THIS PHANTOM BEAST, SWEAR YOU'LL NEVER EAT ANOTHER PIECE OF CHEESE, LATE AT NIGHT.

THE CAT BURGLAR

IS PROWLING AROUND AT THE HOUR OF MIDNIGHT, PAWING THROUGH YOUR STUFF. THE THIEVING MOG IS LOOKING FOR ANYTHING IT CAN FIND. WATCH OUT THERE'S A CAT CROOK ABOUT.

THE HYGIENE PEST

HE MAKES YOU WASH YOUR HANDS AGAIN AND AGAIN. MY HANDS ARE CLEANER THAN A SURGEON'S, MUST I WASH THEM YET AGAIN?

THE TALKING TELLY

IS TALKING TO YOU PERSONALLY; FLASHING YOU MESSAGES ON THE BOX, SENDING YOU ROUND THE TWIST. SWITCH OVER TO THE OTHER SIDE AND GET THE OTHER POINT OF VIEW.

These monsters,
when you look back on them,
they can't hurt you...

THE TIME SNAKE

UNCOILING THE YEARS AND SAYING "YOU'LL HAVE PROBLEMS FOR YEARS AND YEARS!"

THE HYPNOTIC WHEEL

PUTS YOU IN A TRANCE AND TAKES YOU BACK TO YOUR CHILDHOOD, WHERE YOUR PROBLEMS STARTED. YOU WERE FRIGHTENED BY A HYPNOTIC WHEEL.

THE DEATH WISH

TO BE OR NOT TO BE? LIFE'S GOT NOTHING TO OFFER YOU ANY MORE. YOU'VE GOT THE DEATH WISH. R.I.P. REST IN PEACE.

THE UGLY WART

MAKES YOU THINK YOU'RE HORRIBLE AND REPULSIVE. YOU WILL RECOIL WITH HORROR AND SHUDDER EVERY TIME YOU LOOK INTO THE MIRROR AND SEE THE WART APPEAR.

You fear what you can't see. Once you bring fears into the open, they're not so bad...

THE SECRET SPY

A DOUBLE AGENT WHO DIVIDES YOUR MIND IN HALF BY WHISPERING HALF TRUTHS AND LIES INTO YOUR HEAD.

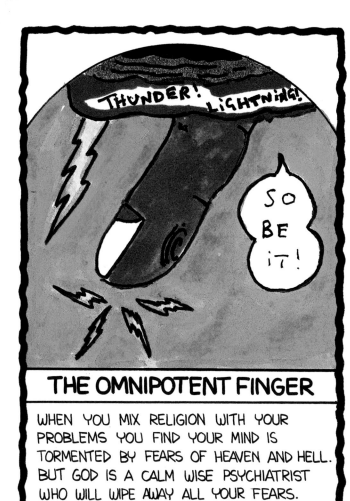

THE OMNIPOTENT FINGER

WHEN YOU MIX RELIGION WITH YOUR PROBLEMS YOU FIND YOUR MIND IS TORMENTED BY FEARS OF HEAVEN AND HELL. BUT GOD IS A CALM WISE PSYCHIATRIST WHO WILL WIPE AWAY ALL YOUR FEARS.

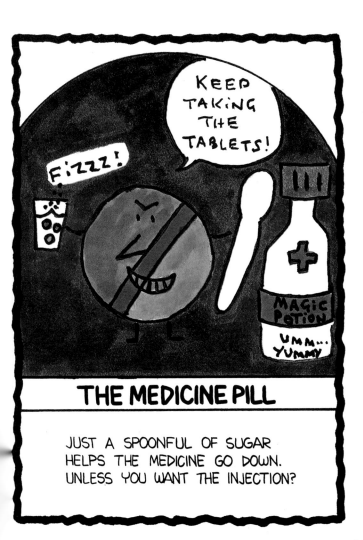

THE MEDICINE PILL

JUST A SPOONFUL OF SUGAR HELPS THE MEDICINE GO DOWN. UNLESS YOU WANT THE INJECTION?

THE LAZY BLOB

IT SAYS "WHY SHOULD I BOTHER?" IT DOES NOTHING ALL DAY EXCEPT WOBBLES LIKE A JELLY.

Think up your own monsters...

Talk about them

Write about them

Draw them

See what comes...

THE FEAR OF DOGS

YOU'RE SCARED OF DOGS. BUT BARKING DOGS NEVER BITE. TELL THAT TO A BARKING DOG.

THE WICKED VILLAIN

THE MUSIC HALL VILLAIN WHO TWISTS HIS MOUSTACHE, TELLING YOU TO DO DARK DEEDS. A BAD EVIL MAN. A THOROUGHLY HORRIBLE VILLAIN.

THE MAGIC HALLUCINATION

NOW YOU SEE IT, NOW YOU DON'T. IS IT A TRICK OF THE EYE? OR THE MAGIC ILLUSION OF THE HALLUCINATION?

THE SANDMAN

FEELING TIRED... YOU CAN'T KEEP YOUR EYES OPEN... ALL YOU WANT TO DO IS SLEEP... ZZZ YOU'VE BEEN CAUGHT BY THE SANDMAN.

NOW SWITCH OFF
THE LIGHT INSIDE YOUR HEAD,
AND GET ON WITH YOUR REAL LIFE.

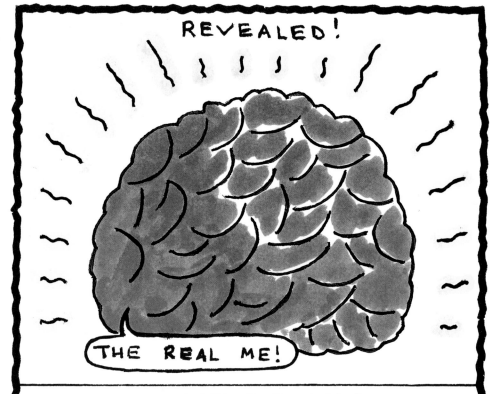

THE BRAIN

ALL THAT'S REALLY INSIDE YOUR HEAD IS YOUR BRAIN. THE MONSTERS DON'T REALLY EXIST. THEY WERE ALL JUST THE FANTASIES OF THE MIND.

AN ILLUSION

THE END

FURTHER CONTACTS

If you have anxieties which are difficult for you to handle on your own, or if you want help to develop new interests, talents and skills, the groups listed below may be able to offer information or support.

Contact your local Council For Voluntary Service for local addresses or for information about voluntary work.

Association for Postnatal Illness.
Institute of Obstetrics & Gynaecology, Queen Charlotte's Hospital, London W6. 081 741 5019

Be Not Anxious.
33 Broadway Ave, Rainham, Kent. ME8 9DB 0634 34262 (1pm-5pm).
Free counselling service by letter & phone for people with agarophobia & anxiety.

Depressives Anonymous.
Mrs P Freya. 36 Chestnut Ave., Beverley, North Humberside, HU17 9QU. Newsletter.

British Association for Counselling.
37a Sheep St., Rugby, Warwickshire. CV21 3BX 0788 78328/9
Can give information on counselling services run by individual counsellors in different areas.

International Stress & Tension Control Society.
The Priory Hospital, Priory Lane, London SW15 5JJ
Promotes better understanding of stress management & tension control. Newsletter.

MIND
22 Harley St., London W1N 2ED 071 637 0741
The national association for mental health. Local branches. Leaflets, books, reports, newsletter.

National Schizophrenia Fellowship.
78-79 Victoria Road, Surbiton, Surrey. KT6 4NS 081 390 3651/2/3.

Portia Trust
Maryport Workspace, Maryport, Cumbria. CA15 8NF 0900 812 114 (day) 0900 812 379 (evenings).
Advice, counselling, phonelink networks. Magazine.

Richmond Fellowship
8 Addison Rd., London W14 8DL 071 603 6373/4/5.
Support, accommodation, counselling. Also provides training & aims to educate the public about mental health issues.

Women's Health Information Centre (WHIC)
52 Featherstone St., London EC1 071 251 6580
(Tues/Thurs 10-4). National information & resource centre for women's health issues.

HEALTHLINE TAPES
Phone 081 980 4848 between 2-7, seven days a week)
26 Acute Anxiety.
82 Anorexia Nervosa.
81 Stress.
202 Agarophobia; what it is & how it is treated.
124 Emotional feelings after childbirth; post-natal depression.
206 Insomnia; how to cope with lack of sleep.
179 Tranquilisers and how to get off them.

RELAXATION AND LEISURE

Age Concern
60 Pitcairn Rd., Mitcham, Surrey. CR4 3LL 081 640 5431
Promotes the welfare of elderly people. Local groups, publications.

Central Council of Physical Recreation
Francis House, Francis St, London SW1P 1DE 071 828 3163
Provides information about 250 sports associations.

Federation of Worker Writers & Community Publishers (FWWCP)
c/o Queenspark Books, 68 Grand Parade, Brighton BN2 2JY 0273 511 916
Provides support & encouragement for working class writing. Local writers' groups. Newsletter.

Keep Fit Association
16 Upper Woburn Place, London WC1H 0QG 071 387 4349
Organises fitness classes. Provides advice on excercise.

Relaxation For Living.
29 Burwood Park Rd., Walton on Thames, Surrey.KT12 5LH
Hold group classes around the UK. Leaflets, tapes, correspondance course.

Spare Tyre
86 Holmleigh Rd., London N16 5PY 081 800 9099
Offers help to women with eating problems. Local groups, talks, telephone advice. Performs shows on aspects of women's health.

Yoga For Health Foundation.
Ickwell Bury, Nr Biggleswade, Beds. SG18 9ES 0767 27271
Promotes yoga for the development of mental & physical well being. Local clubs & centres.

USING A GUIDE TO THE MONSTERS OF THE MIND.

You could use the book as a reader, concentrating on the cartoons and their headings, and the line-broken text on the left hand page.

You could look at the book in two's or three's and concentrate on one page, or one monster, using it to start off discussion.

As well as talking and writing, why not try drawing, painting, photography or making models to express your ideas?

You can use the book to help you understand scary experiences. It is written by someone who's also had some scary experiences. Its pictures give us different ways of exploring our ideas.

You might be able to find new ways of looking at some of the ideas in the book.

You can use this book to take away some of the fear about mental illness, and to help take away the labels that put people down.

Please write with your comments on this material to:

Victor Grenko, c/o Gatehouse Project, St Luke's, Sawley Road, Manchester. M10 8DB

PUBLICATIONS LIST

Gatehouse publishes books written or taped by people who have reading and writing difficulties.

COLLECTED WRITINGS

OPENING TIME: G. Frost, C. Hoy   £25.00   ISBN 0 906253 13 6
A Writing Resource Pack written by students in Basic Education.
341 A4 pages, 14 sections.

JUST LATELY I REALISE   £2.95   ISBN 0 906253 17 9
Women and men who came from the West Indies in the 1950's and
1960's tell stories about their lives.
96 A5 pages.

WHO FEELS IT KNOWS IT   £1.95   ISBN 0 906253 07 1
Writing by students from the West Indies living in Manchester.
26 A5 pages.

TIP OF MY TONGUE   £1.95   ISBN 0 906253 09 8
Women writing about their lives at home and at work.
22 A5 pages.

WHERE DO WE GO FROM HERE   £2.95   ISBN 0 906253 20 9
11 people tell how they survived as adult non-readers in today's world.
80 A5 pages.

DAY IN DAY OUT   £2.95   ISBN 0 906253 19 5
Memories of North Manchester from women in Monsall Hospital.
Oral History.
39 A4 pages.

WHO AM I?   £1.95   ISBN 0 906253 13 16
Writing about women's lives, selected and planned by a women's writers group.
35 A5 pages.

POETRY

YES I LIKE IT   reprint 1991   ISBN 0 906253 16 0
41 poems by new writers. Honest & refreshing, this book is a must for
anyone interested in writing themselves.
84 pages.

BOOKS FOR BEGINNER READERS

JUST MY LUCK   Frances Holden   £1.60   ISBN 0 906253 11 X
A short, funny story. "I should have gone to a wedding..."
16 A5 pages. Large clear print & line-broken.

TOO LATE   Frances Holden   £1.60   ISBN 0 906253 12 8
A visit to the dentist with a difference!
14 A5 pages. Large clear print & line-broken.

KEEP YOUR HAIR ON   Frances Holden   £1.60   ISBN 0 906253 14 4
The evening started in an ordinary way for Frances and Kathleen. Then something unexpected happened....
16 A5 pages. Large clear print & line-broken.

(SPECIAL OFFER PRICE £3.40 FOR PACK OF THREE FRANCES HOLDEN TITLES. ASK FOR '3 BEGINNER READERS'.)

A GOOD LIFE   Alan   £1.60   ISBN 0 906253 00 4
Alan talks about his job and how for once reading problems can be a
positive asset.
12 A5 pages. Large clear print & line-broken.

AUTOBIOGRAPHIES

BAGELS WITH BABUSHKA   Hilda Cohen   £2.95   ISBN 0 906253 31 4
Poet, pensioner and feminist, Hilda Cohen writes of Salford between the wars.
63 A5 pages.

MY WAY OF LIVING   Carol Millbanks   £2.95   ISBN 0 906253 23 3
Extracts from a life. Carol, daughter, friend, worker, organiser and also
physically handicapped from birth.
64 A5 pages.

NEVER IN A LOVING WAY   Josie Byrnes   £1.95   ISBN 0 906253 01 2
In her moving story of childhood, Josie tells of her feelings as a child
struggling to cope with hardship and a lack of love.
33 A5 pages. Told twice, large line-broken print & medium print.

A WOMAN ON HER OWN   Margaret Fulcher   £1.45   ISBN 0 906253 03 9
In five pieces, Margaret describes her life as a woman bringing up a
child on her own.
20 A5 pages. Large print, line-broken.

(Nominated for the Whittakers 'Read Easy' Award.)

THE DAYS I LIVED IN QUEEN STREET, BURY   £1.60   ISBN 0 906253 04
Eric Newsham
It was just one row of old houses, but it was always humming with excitement.
20 A5 pages. Large print, line-broken.

LOCAL PUBLICATIONS

THE BEAUMONT WRITERS GROUP   Various   £1.45   ISBN 0 906253
Described as a 'refreshingly spontaneous insight' (ALBSU)
into the lives of the writers, all of whom suffer from cerebral palsy.
48 A5 pages.

FROM PEN TO PAPER   Various   £1.45   ISBN 0 906253 28 4
Words of experience from an older writers group.
48 A5 pages.

DRAMA

CHIPPING IN AT PRESTWICH   Various   £1.45   ISBN 0 906253 29 2
'Three skilful and amusing short plays' (ALBSU)
36 A5 pages.

NEW TITLE

LISTEN TO ME   Fay   £1.95   ISBN 0 906253 30 6
talking survival
23 A5 pages
"DISTURBING", "MOVING", "POWERFUL", "ACCESSIBLE".
The writer takes the story of a woman looking back on the experience of being sexually abused as a child and goes
on to show her coping with it as an adult. Gatehouse Books is publishing this as a vital part in the struggle to recognise
and make public the long term pain and distress heaped on to those who survive child sexual abuse. It is an account
from which we can all derive hope, and begin to see a way through.
(Nominated for the Arts Council 'Raymond Williams Community Publishing Award'.)

FORTHCOMING TITLES

TELLING TALES

A collection of short stories, poems and plays, written by students in Basic Education. Suitable for a wide range of readers, from the adult beginner to the more advanced.

THEN AND NOW

A Resource Pack for reminiscence work with the elderly.
Written and compiled by Patricia Duffin.
Based on work with the elderly in hospital and sheltered housing, it provides detailed examples and suggestions of ways of encouraging and developing memories. Includes a copy of the 'Day In Day Out' publication.